RUBANK Treasures
for FLUTE

Printable Piano Accompaniments

PLAYBACK+
Speed • Pitch • Balance • Loop

CONTENTS

To access recordings and PDF piano accompaniments, go to:
www.halleonard.com/mylibrary

Enter Code
7721-1956-8699-1074

ISBN 978-1-4803-5240-7

RUBANK®

HAL•LEONARD®
7777 W. BLUEMOUND RD. P.O. BOX 13819 Milwaukee, WI 53213

Copyright ©2018 by HAL LEONARD CORPORATION
International Copyright Secured   All Rights Reserved

Visit Hal Leonard Online at
www.halleonard.com

Barcarole
Op. 30, No. 3

Flute

Ernesto Köhler
Edited by H. Voxman

00121400

Sakura, Sakura
(Cherry Blossoms)

Flute

Japanese Folk Song
Arranged by Harold L. Walters

Pavane pour une Infante Défunte

Flute

Maurice Ravel
Arranged by Harold L. Walters

Meadowlark

Flute

Paul Koepke

Wind in the Pines

Flute

Clair W. Johnson

00121400

Adoration

Flute

Felix Borowski
Arranged by Clair W. Johnson

Allegro agitato

Tempo I

Poplars in the Wind

Flute

Paul Koepke

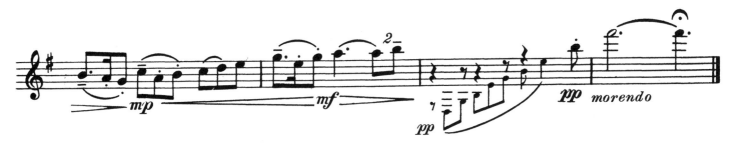

Alleluja

from *Exsultate, Jubilate, K. 165*

Flute

W.A. Mozart
Arranged by Clair W. Johnson

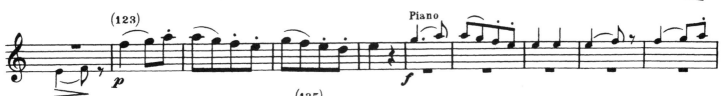

Serenade

Flute

Camille Saint-Saëns
Edited by H. Voxman

00121400

The Dance of Elizabeth

(inspired by Elizabeth I, Queen of England, 1558-1603)

Flute

Clarence E. Hurrell

Three Aquarelles

Flute

I – Hidden Spring

Paul Koepke

II – Heron

III – Dragonfly

00121400

Sonata in F Major

from *Der Getreue Musik-Meister*

Flute

Georg Philipp Telemann
Edited by H. Voxman/Continuo by R.Hervig

* All trills should begin on the beat on the upper auxiliary.

21

00121400

Allegro
from Sonata in B♭ Major

Flute

Paul Koepke